Sauces
Dips &
Dressings

Introduction from Madeline

Greetings fellow traveler,

Whether you are new on the path to wellness or have been on this journey for some time, chances are that you have encountered periods where inspiration is needed to support you in reaching your next level of well-being.

In this fast-paced "grab and go" world, available choices of healthy options are often rather limited. Look no further than most packaged supermarket fare and the abundance of "fast-food" (and I use the word "food" loosely) establishments and it's easy to see how our taste buds are tricked by the deliberate combination of sugar, salt and fat that leaves us unsatisfied and wanting more.

The result of this way of eating is a major contributor to all manner of illness and even early death. According to some estimates, 80% of illness is directly related to poor dietary choices.

As more and more consumers are beginning to connect the dots between their health and the quality of the food they are eating, interest in nutrient-dense foods that are both tasty and satisfying continues to increase. Since I believe everything tastes better with a great sauce, I have created this collection of some of my favorite recipes. All are dairy- and gluten-free, super-healthy and mostly raw for optimal nutrition.

Quality of Ingredients

I strongly recommend buying organic ingredients whenever possible for the highest available nutrient value and the lowest chance of toxic pesticide residue. Since genetically modified foods are either heavily sprayed with (or manufacture their own) bug killers, I urge avoidance of all genetically modified organisms (GMOs). They haven't been properly tested and there is mounting evidence that they are unsafe. In addition, the World Health Organization recently declared that glyphosate, the active ingredient in Roundup™ herbicide, is a "probable carcinogen." Locally-sourced (whenever possible), sustainably-grown, and fair-trade ingredients are the most desirable.

About Essential Oils

Pure essential oils that have been organically grown and properly distilled add an exciting flavor boost to any recipe. The formulas in this book include "essential variations," tips for use of essential oils to add that extra zing to your culinary creations. Remember, quality counts! Since many oils on the market today are synthetic, check to make sure your suppliers' products are pure, undiluted, free of pesticides, contaminants and fillers, and are approved for internal consumption.

Some essential oils are very potent (oregano, ginger, thyme, marjoram, and peppermint are examples). Even one full drop can be overwhelming; that's why some recipes call for a number of "toothpick"-sized amounts. The amount of "1 toothpick" is the quantity that can be transferred by dipping a toothpick in the oil, and then swishing it around with the other ingredients in the recipe.

This book is dedicated to the
many organic farmers, activists,
and volunteers striving to create a
food system that is sustainable
and in harmony with all of life.

Acknowledgments

Mark Eyer, my beloved husband, for his love, unwavering support and dedication to me and to this project. I am also extremely grateful for his photography expertise, technical support, editing and layout skills, as well as his willingness to be one of my primary taste testers.

Royce Richardson, artist and illustrator extraordinare for his creativity, patience, and friendship, and his willingness to be another one of my taste testers.

Dr. DiVanna VaDree for her friendship, spiritual support, and for also allowing me to experiment on her taste buds.

You, the reader, for taking the step to eat healthier and improve your life.

Contents

Almond Dipping Sauce

"Peanut Sauce without the Peanuts"

1/4 cup creamy almond butter
2 medium cloves garlic, crushed
2 tablespoons orange juice
1 tablespoon gluten-free, non-GMO tamari
1 teaspoon Sriracha sauce
1 teaspoon Thai coconut sugar

Using a fork, combine the almond butter, garlic and coconut sugar in a small bowl. One by one, stir in the remaining ingredients.

This sauce is a wonderfully tasty substitute for peanut sauce, which many people have been known to have an allergic reaction to.

Essential variation: Try substituting two tablespoons purified water with two drops pure orange essential oil for the orange juice.

While peanuts are considered the bad boys of the nut family with their history of causing health reactions, almonds, with their fragrant blossoms and nutritional density are often regarded as a symbol of health and beauty.

Food Jail

Almond Umeboshi Plum Sauce

1/2 cup almond butter

1/4 cup lemon juice

1 tablespoon olive oil

1 medium clove garlic, crushed

1/2 teaspoon ginger, minced

1 teaspoon umeboshi plum paste

Blend all ingredients in a small blender jar until well combined. Note: You can also use a stick blender.

Umeboshi is used as a condiment in the macrobiotic diet and has a fruity, salty, sour flavor. These dried plums are believed to support the immune system and aid the body in eliminating toxins.

Essential variation: Add in a drop or two of lemon essential oil for some extra tanginess.

3

There is a belief in traditional Japanese folklore that eating an umeboshi plum before leaving your house helps to ward off calamity and misfortune.

Asian Dipping Sauce

1/2 cup organic, gluten-free tamari
1/4 cup Thai coconut sugar
1/4 cup olive oil
1–2 cloves garlic (to taste)
1 teaspoon ginger, minced
1 dash red pepper flakes

Place all ingredients in your blender and blend until smooth and creamy.

Unused portion can be stored in a sealed container in the fridge for about a week.

Essential variation: 1 or 2 toothpicks* pure ginger essential oil in place of fresh ginger.
*Please see Introduction.

Although tamari is not considered raw, it is gluten-free, unlike its raw cousin, nama shoyu. Be sure to choose organic soy due to the genetic modification of most commercial soybeans.

Baby Bella Sauce

4 cups baby portobello mushrooms
1 cup raw cashews, soaked then rinsed
1 cup coconut milk (unsweetened)
3 tablespoons extra virgin olive oil
2 tablespoons gluten-free, non-GMO tamari
2 tablespoons fresh parsley, chopped
1 tablespoon fresh lemon juice
4 cloves garlic, crushed
1/2 jalapeño pepper (remove seeds for less spice)

Make a marinade with 2 tablespoons tamari, 2 tablespoons olive oil and 2 cloves garlic. Slice and marinate the mushrooms overnight in the fridge.

Combine cashews, coconut milk, remaining olive oil, garlic, lemon, jalapeño and half of the marinated mushrooms in a high-speed blender until creamy. Pour the sauce over your favorite noodles (I prefer kelp or zucchini) and toss. Stir in the remaining mushrooms, top with parsley and serve at room temperature or warmed in a dehydrator.

Essential variation: Try 1 drop of pure lemon essential oil in place of the fresh lemon juice.

Mushrooms, as a species, encompass a very large family. In the case of the cremini mushrooms, they are actually the babies of the fully-matured parents which we know as portobello mushrooms.

Black Turtle Bean Dip

2 cups black beans, cooked and drained
1/2 cup coconut milk
2 tablespoons fresh lime juice
2 medium cloves garlic, crushed
1 teaspoon cumin, ground
1/2 teaspoon pink Himalayan salt
1/4 teaspoon chipotle

Puree all ingredients in a
blender or food processor.
Enjoy with your favorite
crackers, chips, or veggies.

Essential variation: Substitute two drops pure
cumin essential oil for the ground cumin and/or
two drops lime essential oil for fresh lime juice.

Black beans, often referred to as black turtle beans, are believed to have originated in Mexico and South America.

Brazilian Nut Drizzle

1/4 cup (about 10) Brazil nuts

1/4 cup purified water

2 tablespoons chickpea miso

2 tablespoons fresh lemon juice

2 tablespoons Thai coconut sugar

1 clove garlic

Blend all ingredients in a high-speed blender until smooth and creamy. Enjoy as a dip or drizzled over your favorite entrée.

Essential variation: Substitute 2 tablespoons purified water and 2 drops pure lemon essential oil for the fresh lemon juice. For extra zip, consider adding in a couple of drops of pure orange essential oil. Yum.

Cardamom Almond Milk

1 cup raw organic almonds

5 cups purified water

1/2 teaspoon pure vanilla powder

1/4 teaspoon cardamom, ground

Soak almonds for 6–8 hours in 2 cups purified water. Drain and rinse a couple of times until the water is clear. Place almonds in a high-speed blender. Add 2 cups of water and blend until somewhat liquified. Add remaining cup of water, vanilla and cardamom. Blend again.

Strain through a nut milk bag with a bowl underneath, gently squeezing until the pulp is dry. Reserve pulp for use in other recipes such as crackers, croutons, cookies, etc. Store in the freezer until you are ready to use. Milk will keep in an airtight container in the fridge for about five days.

Essential variation: Use 1 drop pure cardamom essential oil in place of the ground cardamom.

According to folklore, cardamom was believed to be an aphrodisiac and was frequently found in love charms and perfumes. It had a stronger effect on males than females.

14

Chimichurri Sauce

2 cups Italian flat leaf parsley, packed (about 1 bunch)
1/2 cup extra virgin olive oil
3–4 medium cloves garlic, pressed
1 tablespoon fresh lemon juice
1 tablespoon shallot, minced
1/4 teaspoon red pepper flakes
1/8 teaspoon pink Himalayan salt

Pulse parsley, garlic, lemon and shallot
in a food processor until well combined
and still slightly chunky. Avoid over-processing
or it will turn to mush. Transfer mixture into
a bowl and stir in olive oil,
salt and pepper.

Essential variation: Consider substituting 2 drops of
pure lemon essential oil for the fresh lemon juice.

A story is told that Argentinean gauchos created the first Chimichurri as a sauce for the food they cooked over their nightly campfires during long trips into the wild when they would hunt for feral cattle.

Cranberry Orange Dressing

2 cups cranberries (fresh or frozen)

1/2 cup extra virgin olive oil

1/4 cup purified water

1/4 cup fresh orange juice

1/4 cup Thai coconut sugar

2 medium cloves garlic

1/2 teaspoon pink Himalayan salt

Place cranberries in a high-speed blender. Add water, orange juice, coconut sugar, garlic and salt and blend until well combined. Use a funnel to drizzle in olive oil while blending on low speed.

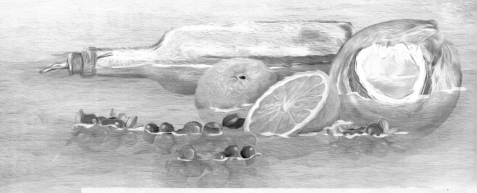

Essential variation: In place of orange juice, increase water by 1/4 cup and add in 4 drops pure orange essential oil.

Cranberry Pear Relish

2 cups fresh cranberries
1 Bartlett pear
1 satsuma tangerine
1 tablespoon fresh ginger, grated
2 teaspoons Ceylon cinnamon

Place all ingredients in a high-speed blender or food processor and pulse until slightly chunky, but not watery.

While cranberry relish commonly graces many holiday tables, its use goes way beyond that. Leftovers can be baked into muffins, poured over salads, frozen in ice cube trays for use in smoothies, or served as an accompaniment to sandwiches.

Essential variation: Replace fresh tangerine fruit with one drop pure tangerine essential oil and a tablespoon of water if needed.

Creamy Persimmon Dressing

1 persimmon

1/2 cup cashews, soaked and rinsed

1/4 cup orange juice

2 tablespoons apple cider vinegar

1 tablespoon maple syrup

1 tablespoon shallot, minced

1 tablespoon purified water

Place all ingredients in a high-speed blender and blend until smooth and creamy.

Essential variation: Use 1/4 cup purified water with 2–3 drops pure orange essential oil in lieu of the orange juice.

In Korean folklore it is said that dried persimmons have unique properties which were thought to scare away tigers.

Creamy Sun-dried Tomato Vinaigrette

1/2 cup olive oil

1/4 cup sun-dried tomatoes, rehydrated, rinsed and
well drained

1/4 cup purified water

2 tablespoons apple cider vinegar

1 medium clove garlic, pressed

salt and pepper to taste

Optional: basil, parsley, thyme or herbs of your choice.

Blend sun-dried tomatoes, purified water, apple cider
vinegar and garlic in a small blender jar. Continue blending
while slowly adding in the olive oil.
Add salt and pepper to taste, and
a pinch of your favorite herbs if
desired. You can also use an
immersion (a.k.a. stick) blender
to combine and emulsify
the ingredients.

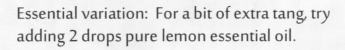

Essential variation: For a bit of extra tang, try
adding 2 drops pure lemon essential oil.

Crushed Pineapple Dipping Sauce

2 cups of pineapple chunks

1/2 cup cilantro

2 tablespoons fresh lime juice

1/2 teaspoon fresh red pepper

pinch pink Himalayan salt

Blend together all ingredients to your desired consistency. Smooth or slightly chunky—you decide!

Essential variation: Instead of fresh lime, try substituting two tablespoons purified water and two drops pure lime essential oil.

Although the Hawaiian Islands are famous
for their production of pineapples,
the first pineapple plants were
imported from Brazil and
Paraguay around 1527.

Dairy-free Tzatziki Sauce

2 cups cucumber

1/2 cup Brazil nuts

1/4 cup Italian parsley, packed

3 tablespoons lemon juice

2 tablespoons tahini

2 large mint leaves

1 small clove garlic

Slice cucumber lengthwise so that the seedy center remains. (Set this part aside to enjoy as a snack). Chop the outer portion into chunks and place in your high-speed blender. Add the remaining ingredients and blend until smooth and creamy.

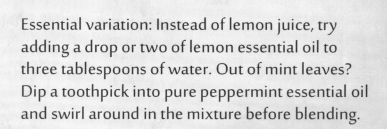

Essential variation: Instead of lemon juice, try adding a drop or two of lemon essential oil to three tablespoons of water. Out of mint leaves? Dip a toothpick into pure peppermint essential oil and swirl around in the mixture before blending.

Greek
Cafe

No Cows
Allowed

This light and deliciously raw recipe is a dairy-free alternative to the traditional Greek tzatziki sauce, which is made with yogurt, cucumber and garlic. Try it on falafels or as a dip.

Dressing for Summer

1/2 cup fresh-squeezed lime juice

2 small cloves garlic, pressed

1 tablespoon Thai coconut sugar

1/4 jalapeño pepper, minced

pinch pink Himalayan salt

Place all ingredients in a small blender jar and blend until smooth.

This light citrus dressing tastes great when tossed with julienned jicama and fennel. Add in a bit of cilantro and halved cherry tomatoes and, voila— you've got the perfect summer salad!

Essential variation: Mix in 1 toothpick (see Introduction) pure lemongrass essential oil for a slight flavor twist.

30

Dressing in Dill

1 cup organic cashews

1 cup purified water

1/4 cup fresh dill

2 medjool dates, pitted

2 tablespoons apple cider vinegar

2 tablespoons fresh-squeezed lemon juice

2 tablespoons fresh orange juice

Soak cashews in purified water for 6–8 hours and rinse well. Add cashews, water, and other ingredients *except* the dill to a high-speed blender. Blend until smooth and creamy. Add dill and pulse briefly.

Essential variation: Substitute 2 drops pure lemon and/or orange essential oil in 2 tablespoons purified water for the fresh lemon or orange juice.

Eggplant Caponata

1 medium eggplant, peeled (about 4 cups)
2 roma tomatoes, diced
1/2 sweet onion, diced
1/2 cup pitted Kalamata olives, rinsed and chopped
1/2 cup pitted green olives, rinsed and chopped
1/2 cup (packed) Italian parsley, finely chopped
1/2 cup capers, rinsed
2 stalks celery, diced (about 1 cup)
2 tablespoons extra virgin olive oil
2 teaspoons pink Himalayan salt
1 teaspoon dried oregano
1/2 teaspoon white pepper

Cut eggplant into 1/4" chunks. Place in a colander with a bowl underneath. Sprinkle with salt. Toss until well-coated and set aside for 30 minutes with a plate on top to drain excess moisture.

Rinse, pat dry, and saute eggplant briefly in olive oil. Dice tomatoes. Strain excess liquid and set in a medium bowl. Add remaining ingredients and toss to combine well.

In the 1700s, early European versions of eggplant were smaller, and yellow or white in color. They looked a bit like goose or hen's eggs, which led to the name "eggplant."

Essential variation: Substitute 1 toothpick (see Introduction) pure marjoram essential oil for the oregano. Similar in flavor, it is milder and sweeter. Add it to the olive oil for more even distribution.

Faux Russian Dressing
New York Style

1 cup raw organic almonds,
    soaked, rinsed & peeled
1 cup Roma tomatoes, diced
2 sun-dried tomatoes,
    soaked and rinsed (optional)*
1/2 cup purified water
1/2 cup olive oil
3 tablespoons dill pickle, chopped
2 tablespoons fresh lemon juice
1 tablespoon apple cider vinegar
2 medium cloves garlic, pressed
2 teaspoons Thai coconut sugar
1 teaspoon Herbamare® seasoning
1/4 teaspoon dry mustard

Blend all ingredients except pickle in a high-speed blender. Stir in pickle with a spoon and transfer to a glass jar with a tight-fitting lid. Keeps for approximately 5 days in the fridge.

*If using sun-dried tomatoes, be sure to rinse well to remove excess salt.

This recipe is a tasty alternative to the classic Russian dressing of my youth. Consider giving it a try on the salad or sandwich of your choice.

Russian Dressing is not, and never has been, a Russian recipe. Unknown in Russia, it was invented in America, most likely in New York sometime in the late 1800s.

Hail Señor Caesar

1/2 cup macadamia nuts

1/2 cup purified water

1/2 cup olive oil

1/4 cup fresh lemon juice

3 teaspoons capers, rinsed well

2 medium cloves garlic, pressed

1 teaspoon prepared mustard

Blend all ingredients *except* olive oil and capers in a high-speed blender. Slowly drizzle in olive oil while continuing to blend. Stir in capers.

This dressing tastes delicious in a salad made of chopped kale and napa cabbage.

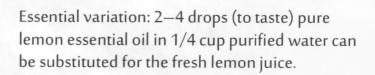

Essential variation: 2–4 drops (to taste) pure lemon essential oil in 1/4 cup purified water can be substituted for the fresh lemon juice.

Although the Caesar salad is often associated with the Caesars of Rome, it was actually created in Tijuana, Mexico by a restaurateur named Caesar Cardini who, finding himself low on supplies, threw together some random ingredients and presto, the Caesar salad was born!

38

Herb Vinaigrette

3/4 cup extra virgin olive oil

1/4 cup purified water

1/4 cup apple cider vinegar

1 small clove garlic, pressed

1 tablespoon fresh basil, minced

1 teaspoon Dijon mustard

1/2 teaspoon dried Italian herbs

salt and pepper to taste

Place all ingredients in a glass jar with tight-fitting lid and shake thoroughly until well combined.

Store leftover dressing in the fridge for up to two days.

It's best to choose raw, unfiltered, organic apple cider vinegar that contains "the mother." This will ensure that the enzymes and minerals remain intact rather than being destroyed by processing, filtration or heating.

Vinaigrette is an emulsion of vinegar and some form of oil, such as olive or other high-quality oil. Note: I recommend avoiding canola oil.

Holy Guacamole

1 large Hass avocado
1 Roma tomato, finely chopped
2 tablespoons red onion, minced
2 tablespoons fresh cilantro, chopped
2 tablespoons fresh lime juice
1 tablespoon jalapeño pepper, minced
1 clove garlic, pressed
1/2 teaspoon pink Himalayan salt
1/2 teaspoon cumin, ground

Mash the avocado in a small bowl or mortar (if you have one). Mix in the lime juice; the citrus will help to keep the avocado from turning brown. Next, stir in the onion, garlic, jalapeño and salt. Add the tomato and cilantro last, mixing gently.

Essential variation: Substitute 1 tablespoon water with 3 drops pure lime essential oil for the lime juice or 1 drop cumin oil for the ground cumin.

Enjoy with raw crackers or serve as a veggie dip. You can purchase raw crackers at many natural grocery stores or make them yourself in a dehydrator.

Lemon Caper Relish

1 cup cucumber, seeded and finely chopped

1/4 cup red onion, finely chopped

1/4 cup fresh lemon juice

2 tablespoons capers, rinsed well to remove excess salt

1 tablespoon extra virgin olive oil

1 teaspoon Thai coconut sugar

1/4 teaspoon pink Himalayan salt

Place cucumber, onion and capers in a small bowl, then set aside. Blend together lemon juice, olive oil, coconut sugar and salt. Pour over cucumber mixture and stir until well combined. Refrigerate for several hours or overnight. We enjoy this smothered over our favorite veggie burgers.

Essential variation: For some extra zing, add in 3 drops pure lemon essential oil and stir well. This is our favorite preparation.

Although prized by people, lemons are actually a natural repellent for most animals, insects and reptiles. There is even an old wive's tale that says, if you have recently eaten a lemon, a snake will find you distasteful and not want to bite you.

Macadamia 'n Cheese

1/2 cup raw macadamia nuts

1/4 cup nutritional yeast

6 tablespoons purified water

1 tablespoon fresh lemon juice

1/4 teaspoon pink Himalayan salt

Blend all ingredients until smooth and creamy. Yes, it really is that simple!

Tastes great tossed with veggie noodles or anything you enjoy with saucy cheese.

Nutritional yeast is often referred to as a superfood due to its abundance of vitamins, minerals and protein. It is usually grown from sugar cane but can also come from beet molasses.

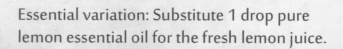

Essential variation: Substitute 1 drop pure lemon essential oil for the fresh lemon juice.

Macadamia nut trees are native to Australia. It is believed that they were first harvested by the Aboriginal people that still inhabit the Australian rain forests.

Moroccan Mama's
Minute Marinade

1/2 cup extra virgin olive oil
1/4 cup preserved lemons, sliced
1/4 cup flat leaf parsley, packed
2 medium cloves garlic, crushed
1 teaspoon fresh ginger, diced

Rinse preserved lemons prior to
slicing in order to remove excess salt.
Place all ingredients *except* olive oil in
a high-speed blender and blend until
smooth and creamy. Slowly
drizzle in olive oil to emulsify,
then saute or warm
briefly in a dehydrator.
Marinate some
fresh
veggies
in this
light and
delicious sauce.

Preserved lemons are lemons that have been pickled with
salt and their own juices, and stored in a canning jar.

Essential variation: For some extra lemony flavor,
add in 2 drops pure lemon essential oil.

48

Mushroom Marinade

4 tablespoons hemp oil

2 tablespoons fresh lemon juice

2 tablespoons shallots, diced

1 clove garlic, minced

1 tablespoon non-GMO verified, gluten-free tamari

1 tablespoon each, fresh parsley & rosemary, minced

Place all ingredients in a jar with a tight-fitting lid and shake vigorously. Pour over fresh veggies and let marinate for a couple of hours.

Tip: Marinating in a dehydrator at 110 degrees F will allow the vegetables to warm and soften.

Essential variation: Substitute 2 drops pure lemon essential oil and 2 tablespoons purified water for lemon juice. No fresh rosemary on hand? In its place you can use 1 toothpick (see Introduction) of rosemary essential oil.

The process of marinating was created for the purpose of preserving food by using sea salt to make a brine for soaking or pickling a variety
of ingredients.

Open Sesame

Tahini Sauce

1 cup raw tahini

3/4 cup fresh lemon juice

1/4 cup purified water

2 medium cloves garlic, crushed

1 tablespoon non-GMO soy sauce

1 tablespoon Thai coconut sugar

1/2 teaspoon dried thyme

Blend all ingredients in a
high-speed blender until creamy.
This quick and easy recipe tastes
great and the tahini is loaded
with nutrition.

Essential variation: Replace dried thyme with one
toothpick (see Introduction) pure thyme essential oil.

The saying "Open Sesame" from *Alibaba and the Forty Thieves,* was actually inspired by the fact that it is not uncommon for ripe sesame pods to burst open when they are picked.

Pea~vocado Dip

1 cup peas, fresh or frozen

1/2 ripe avocado

1/4 cup fresh parsley, packed

2 tablespoons lemon juice

1 teaspoon serrano pepper, minced

1 medium clove garlic, pressed

1/2 teaspoon pink Himalayan salt

Pulse all ingredients in a food processor until well combined and slightly chunky. Adjust salt and serrano pepper to taste.

Note: If using frozen peas, leave out on your kitchen counter briefly until thawed.

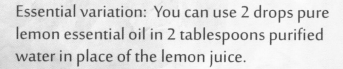

Essential variation: You can use 2 drops pure lemon essential oil in 2 tablespoons purified water in place of the lemon juice.

There is an old wives' tale that if a woman opens a peapod and finds exactly nine peas inside, she can hang that peapod over her front door and the next man to enter will be her future husband.

Peach Ketchup

3 tablespoons sun-dried tomatoes,
 rehydrated, rinsed, and chopped

2 Roma tomatoes, chopped

1/2 cup fresh peaches, chopped

2 tablespoons apple cider vinegar

1 tablespoon purified water

1 teaspoon chia powder

1/2 teaspoon pink Himalayan salt

1/4 teaspoon onion powder

1 small clove garlic

Blend all ingredients in a high-speed blender until smooth.

You can purchase chia powder or you can make your own by grinding chia seeds in a coffee grinder.

Essential variation: Since chia is being used as a thickener, feel free to substitute psyllium powder.

According to Pueblo lore, those who ingested a large quantity of a particular variety of tomato seeds would be blessed with sacred visions and the powers of divination.

Pesto a la Basilisk

1 cup fresh basil, packed

1 cup fresh spinach, packed

2 medium cloves garlic, crushed

6 tablespoons extra virgin olive oil

1/4 cup brazil nuts

1/2 teaspoon pink Himalayan salt

Process all ingredients in a food processor until smooth, or leave slightly chunky if you prefer. Unused portion will keep in the fridge for a few days or may be frozen.

When it comes to pesto, the combinations are endless. I've made this recipe with walnuts and it's equally delicious and nutritious. You are invited to be creative with whatever you have on hand.

According to Greek mythology, basil derives its name from the terrifying basilisk—a half-lizard, half-dragon creature with a fatal piercing stare. The medicinal application of a basil leaf was considered to be a mystical cure against the bite or even the deadly stare of the creature.

Pistachio Coconut Cream Sauce

1 cup + 2 tablespoons raw pistachio nut meat

1/2 cup pure coconut milk

1/2 cup purified water

2 tablespoons fresh lime juice

1 medium clove garlic, crushed

1 teaspoon cumin, ground

1/2 teaspoon chili powder

1/2 teaspoon pink Himalayan salt

Set aside 2 tablespoons of pistachios and blend remaining ingredients until smooth and creamy. For a thinner sauce, add a bit more water. Crush the pistachios you set aside and sprinkle on top of your completed dish.

Essential variation: Substitute 2 drops pure lime essential oil for the fresh lime, and/or one drop pure cumin essential oil for the ground cumin.

Enjoy this velvety dairy-free sauce tossed with your favorite noodles. Due to its richness, a lighter noodle such a spiralized zucchini or kelp would be a great choice. If you don't own a spiralizer, you can use a potato peeler.

Plato's Hummus

1-1/2 cups zucchini, peeled and rough chopped

1 cup cooked garbanzo beans, well-drained

1/4 cup raw tahini

1/4 cup fresh lemon juice

3 tablespoons sun-dried tomato,
    rehydrated, rinsed, and well-drained

3 medium cloves garlic, crushed

2 tablespoons extra-virgin olive oil

1 teaspoon ground cumin

1/2 teaspoon pink Himalayan salt

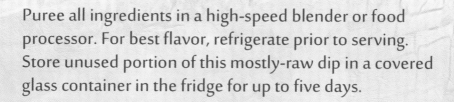

Puree all ingredients in a high-speed blender or food processor. For best flavor, refrigerate prior to serving. Store unused portion of this mostly-raw dip in a covered glass container in the fridge for up to five days.

Essential variation: Substitute two drops of cumin essential oil for the ground cumin. So delicious!

Hidden within the great philosophical writings of Plato and Socrates are passages that tell about hummus and its many health benefits.

Pomegranate Citrus Dressing

1 cup fresh pomegranate arils (seeds)

1/4 cup fresh Italian parsley

1/4 purified water

1/4 cup olive oil

1 small clove garlic

1/2 cup fresh orange juice

Blend all ingredients *except* olive oil in a high-speed blender.

Continue blending and drizzle in the oil gradually so it emulsifies.

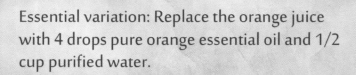

Essential variation: Replace the orange juice with 4 drops pure orange essential oil and 1/2 cup purified water.

Sometimes in Turkey, after her marriage ceremony, the bride throws a pomegranate on the ground. The number of seeds that fall out are believed to foretell how many children she will have.

Puttanesca Sauce

4 cups Roma tomatoes, cut into medium-sized chunks

1 cup sun-dried tomatoes, soaked and rinsed

1/4 cup extra virgin olive oil

1/2 cup pitted Kalamata olives, halved

2 tablespoons capers, rinsed

2 tablespoons shallot, minced

4 medium cloves garlic, crushed

1 tablespoon fresh basil, finely chopped

1/2 teaspoon red pepper flakes

zest of 1 small lemon

Pulse all ingredients *except* basil in a blender or food processor. Slather sauce over your favorite noodles and sprinkle basil on top. Spiralized zucchini or kelp noodles are my go-to.

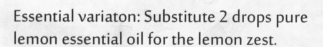

Essential variaton: Substitute 2 drops pure lemon essential oil for the lemon zest.

In Italian, *puttanesca* refers to "the way the ladies of the night would make it." Although no one really knows the origin of this name, it has been a commonly known dish for over a hundred years.

Raw Vegan Barbecue Sauce

1 cup sun-dried tomatoes, soaked and rinsed
6 tablespoons purified water
1 tablespoon apple cider vinegar
1 tablespoon fresh lemon juice
1 tablespoon Thai coconut sugar
1 teaspoon mesquite powder
1 clove garlic, pressed
1 teaspoon onion powder
1/4 teaspoon pink Himalayan salt
1/4 teaspoon chipotle seasoning
1/4 teaspoon cracked white pepper

Blend all ingredients in a small blender jar, adjusting water to your desired consistency and seasonings to suit your taste buds.

Tastes great on raw (dehydrated) or cooked veggie burgers, veggie skewers and raw sandwiches.

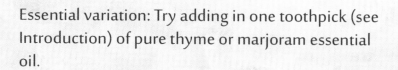

Essential variation: Try adding in one toothpick (see Introduction) of pure thyme or marjoram essential oil.

Red Bell Pepper and Cashew Dressing

1/2 cup cashews, soaked and rinsed

1/4 red bell pepper

1/4 cup fresh orange juice

1 clove garlic

1/4 jalapeño pepper

1 tablespoon apple cider vinegar

1 tablespoon lemon juice

1/4 teaspoon pink Himalayan salt

Soak cashews in purified water for 6–8 hours and rinse well. Add cashews and other ingredients *except* the dill to high-speed blender or food processor. Blend until smooth and creamy. Add dill and pulse.

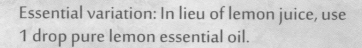

Essential variation: In lieu of lemon juice, use 1 drop pure lemon essential oil.

When Christopher Columbus brought back his newly-discovered fruits from Mexico, he unwittingly named them "peppers" because some of them were hot, resembling the peppercorn spice from India. Today the fruit and the spice have the same name, even though the two species are completely unrelated.

Royce's Cargo Curry

1 pear, seeds and core removed

2 tablespoons fresh lime juice

1/2 cup ground hemp hearts (shelled hemp seeds)

1/4 cup olive oil

2 teaspoons ground turmeric

2 teaspoons ground coriander

2 teaspoons non-GMO tamari

1/2 teaspoon chile powder

1/2 teaspoon ground cumin

1/2 teaspoon ground mustard seed

1 medium clove garlic

Blend all ingredients in a high-speed blender. Serve warmed with your favorite grains or veggies. Unused portion keeps in the fridge for a couple of days.

Essential variation: Substitute 1 drop cumin essential oil for the ground cumin.

It is believed that curry originated in India and was a blend of turmeric, garlic and ginger. As trade routes were established across Asia, numerous cultures added their own regional spices, creating hundreds of curry blends.

Salsa Dip Fiesta

2 Roma tomatoes

1 cup pineapple

1 cup mango

3 tablespoons shallot

3 tablespoons cilantro, chopped

2 tablespoons fresh lime juice

1/2 serrano pepper

pinch pink Himalayan salt

Dice tomatoes, pineapple, mango, shallot and pepper. Place in a medium-sized bowl, add in the lime juice, salt and cilantro. Toss well.

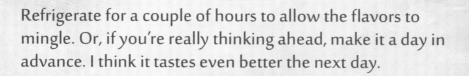

Refrigerate for a couple of hours to allow the flavors to mingle. Or, if you're really thinking ahead, make it a day in advance. I think it tastes even better the next day.

Essential variation: 2 tablespoons pure lime essential oil can be used in lieu of the lime juice.

Salsa music and dancing originated in Cuba, and is the blending of African drum rhythms and Spanish flamenco guitar. Salsa, the condiment, can be traced back to the culinary traditions of the Aztec, Mayan, and Incan civilizations.

Sesame Marinade

1/4 cup gluten-free tamari (non-GMO)

1/4 cup purified water

2 tablespoons rice vinegar

2 tablespoons sesame oil

1 tablespoon Thai coconut sugar

1/4 teaspoon black sesame seeds, ground

Blend all ingredients in a high-speed blender. Store unused portion is a sealed glass container for up to 5 days.

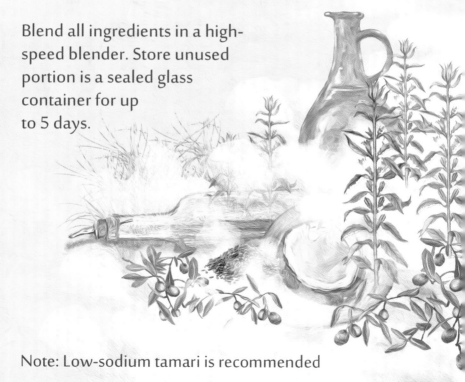

Note: Low-sodium tamari is recommended

Essential alternative: For a flavor twist, try adding two drops pure lime essential oil.

A tale is told that the Earth was created by
two Assyrian gods while they were sharing
a bottle of sesame wine.

Spicy Peanut Sauce

1/2 cup powdered organic peanut butter

3 tablespoons purified water

2 tablespoons coconut milk

2 teaspoons mirin

1 teaspoon Thai coconut sugar

1 small clove garlic, crushed

1/2 teaspoon fresh ginger, minced

1/4 teaspoon cayenne

1/4 teaspoon pink Himalayan salt

Optional: a few crushed raw peanuts

Blend all ingredients (except crushed peanuts if using) in a small blender jar or use an immersion blender.

Essential variations: Add one drop lime essential oil or a squirt of fresh lime. Fresh peanuts are much higher in fat than the powdered form, however you can use them if you prefer.

Any self-respecting peanut will tell you that they are most certainly a bean and not a nut. Like most legumes, peanuts grow on a vine, and like a potato, the actual harvest grows under the soil.

BEAN MANOR

Nut House

Strawberry Jammin'

1 cup fresh organic strawberries

1/4 cup fresh orange juice

2 tablespoons chia seeds

1 teaspoon Thai coconut sugar

Place all ingredients in a small blender jar and blend until smooth.

Chia seeds are a wonderful thickener since they absorb liquid at approximately ten times their volume. They are loaded with nutrition, are a complete source of protein, are high in soluble fiber, and have a pleasant, mild flavor.

Essential variation: Substitute 2 drops pure orange essential oil and 2 (or more) tablespoons purified water in place of the fresh orange juice.

80

Strawberry Poppy Seed Dressing

1 cup purified water

1/2 cup macadamia nuts

4 medium organic strawberries, hulled

2 tablespoons extra virgin olive oil

2 tablespoons poppy seeds

1 tablespoon apple cider vinegar

1 teaspoon mustard powder

1/4 teaspoon pink Himalayan salt

1/4 teaspoon onion powder

Place all ingredients in a high-speed blender and blend until smooth. The macadamia nuts give this dressing a wonderfully creamy texture. Tastes best when chilled for an hour or two prior to serving.

Essential variation: The flavors of pure orange and tangerine essential oils lend themselves well to this recipe. Add a couple of drops and see for yourself.

Poppies are recognized in herbal medicine for their sedative properties, as Dorothy and her friends discovered.

Sunflower Spread

3 cups celery, chopped

2 cups sunflower seeds, soaked 2–4 hours, then rinsed

1/2 bunch fresh parsley, lower stems removed

1/3 cup extra virgin olive oil

1/4 cup fresh-squeezed lemon juice

2 scallions, chopped

2 medium cloves garlic, pressed

1/2 teaspoon pink Himalayan salt

Place all ingredients in a food processor and process until well-combined, stopping occasionally to scrape the inside of the container.

Enjoy immediately or store in a glass container in the fridge for up to 3 days. This recipe is especially tasty when served on collard greens, celery sticks or raw crackers.

Essential variation: You can easily replace the fresh lemon juice with 1/4 cup of purified water and a few drops of pure lemon essential oil.

A superstition is held that when you are seeking
the truth about a particular situation, it
will be revealed to you during the
night if you place a sunflower
under your bed.

Sweet Potato Spread

2 cups sweet potatoes, baked

1/2 cup coconut milk

1 large clove garlic, pressed

1" piece ginger, minced

1/4 teaspoon pink Himalayan salt

Cool sweet potatoes, remove skin and cut into medium-sized chunks.

Place all ingredients in a food processor or high-speed blender and combine until smooth and creamy.

Enjoy this spread on your favorite crackers or wraps. It also makes a tasty and satisfying dip for celery and cucumbers.

Essential variation: Add in two drops orange essential oil and mix until well combined.

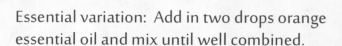

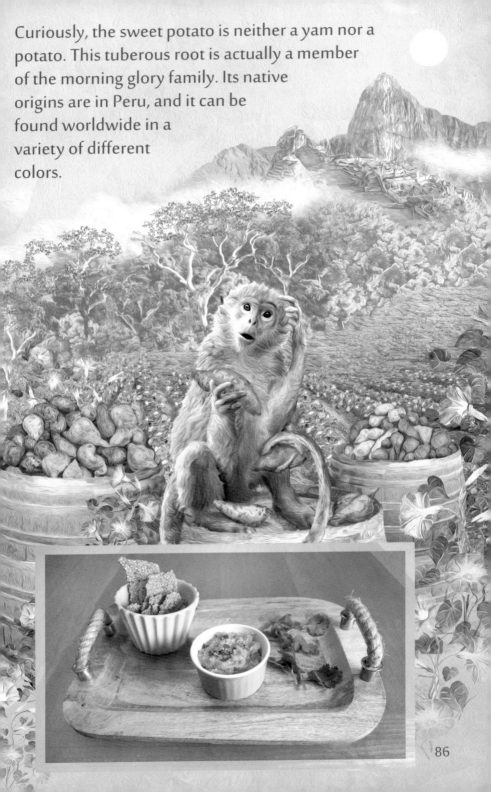

Curiously, the sweet potato is neither a yam nor a potato. This tuberous root is actually a member of the morning glory family. Its native origins are in Peru, and it can be found worldwide in a variety of different colors.

86

Tangy Shallot Dressing

1/4 cup purified water

3 tablespoons extra virgin olive oil

2 tablespoons apple cider vinegar

1 tablespoon shallot, minced

1 teaspoon Dijon mustard

1 teaspoon coconut sugar

salt & pepper to taste

In a small mixing bowl combine the water, cider vinegar, Dijon and coconut sugar. Slowly whisk in the olive oil. Mix in the shallots.

Store unused portion in the fridge in a glass container with a tight-fitting lid. It should keep for about 5 days.

This recipe can be made using a stick blender or you can shake in a mason jar if that's what you've got handy.

Essential variation: For a little extra zip, try adding a couple of drops of pure tangerine essential oil.

Early American folklore tells of a rabbit that tricks a man into releasing it from a trap, saying that a big black "cat" with a stripe down its back is responsible for stealing the man's shallots. When the man grabs a skunk and the skunk retaliates, the rabbit calls out, saying, "The cat has bad breath from eating your shallots."

Tasty Tapenade

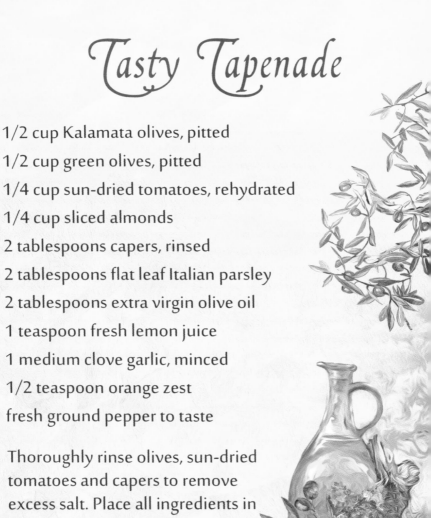

1/2 cup Kalamata olives, pitted

1/2 cup green olives, pitted

1/4 cup sun-dried tomatoes, rehydrated

1/4 cup sliced almonds

2 tablespoons capers, rinsed

2 tablespoons flat leaf Italian parsley

2 tablespoons extra virgin olive oil

1 teaspoon fresh lemon juice

1 medium clove garlic, minced

1/2 teaspoon orange zest

fresh ground pepper to taste

Thoroughly rinse olives, sun-dried tomatoes and capers to remove excess salt. Place all ingredients in a food processor and pulse until well combined.

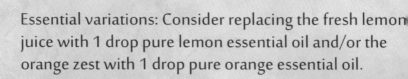

Essential variations: Consider replacing the fresh lemon juice with 1 drop pure lemon essential oil and/or the orange zest with 1 drop pure orange essential oil.

The *Olive Tree of Vouves*, on the island of Crete, is known to be one of the oldest living trees. At an estimated age of 3,000 years, this tree is still bearing fruit and going strong.

Thai Coconut Curry a la Mango

2 fresh mangoes, peeled & chopped

1 cup coconut milk

1 cup cashews, soaked 6—8 hours

2—4 tablespoons purified water

2 tablespoons lime juice

2 tablespoons curry powder (your favorite blend)

pinch pink Himalayan salt

Place all ingredients in a high-speed blender and blend until smooth and creamy. Add water one tablespoon at a time until you achieve your desired consistency.

Tastes great mixed with shredded veggies and served on a cabbage leaf.

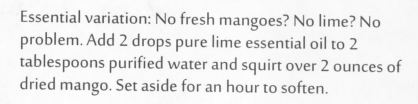

Essential variation: No fresh mangoes? No lime? No problem. Add 2 drops pure lime essential oil to 2 tablespoons purified water and squirt over 2 ounces of dried mango. Set aside for an hour to soften.

While Indian cooking often utilizes ghee to make curry, Thai curries generally incorporate some form of coconut oil or coconut milk.

It is believed that the mango tree originated in eastern India, later spreading throughout the world by travelers who carried the seeds. Legend has it that the Buddha meditated under a shady mango tree.

Vegan Sandwich Spread

1 cup raw almonds, soaked, rinsed and peeled
1 cup purified water
1/2 cup extra virgin olive oil
1/4 cup fresh lemon juice
1/4 cup fresh parsley
1 tablespoon apple cider vinegar
2 teaspoons Thai coconut sugar
1 teaspoon pink Himalayan salt

Blend all ingredients *except* olive oil in a small, powerful blender jar until smooth and creamy. Slowly drizzle in the olive oil as you continue to blend to emulsify.

This fresh and light sandwich spread tastes great on raw crackers and topped with fresh veggies.

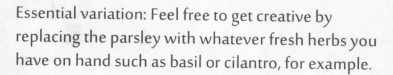

Essential variation: Feel free to get creative by replacing the parsley with whatever fresh herbs you have on hand such as basil or cilantro, for example.

Veggie Herbal Basting Sauce

1/2 cup extra virgin olive oil
1 tablespoon fresh oregano
1 tablespoon fresh parsley
1 tablespoon fresh sage
1 tablespoon fresh thyme
1 teaspoon red pepper flakes
1 medium clove garlic, crushed

Mince fresh herbs and place in a glass jar with a tight-fitting lid. Add in garlic, red pepper flakes and olive oil. Make sure lid is securely fastened and shake until well combined. Allow flavors to meld for at least one hour prior to using.

Note: The herbs selected for this blend were chosen specifically for their flavor profile with vegetables.

Essential variation: A tiny bit (maybe one toothpick) of pure oregano essential oil can substitute for the fresh oregano. It's very strong, so don't overdo it.

Many garden herbs can also be grown in the house if you
have a brightly-lit window and enough space for
the plants to flourish.

Waldorf Spread

1 green apple, chopped

1 cup celery, chopped

1 cup walnuts

2 tablespoons fresh parsley, chopped (for garnish)

1 tablespoon Vegan Sandwich Spread (p. 93)

2 teaspoons fresh lemon juice

salt & pepper to taste

Place celery and apple in food processor. Squirt with lemon. Add in walnuts and pulse until slightly chunky.

Pour into a medium-sized mixing bowl. Stir in almond spread. Add salt and pepper and garnish with fresh parsley. Serve with gluten-free crackers or atop fresh veggies.

Essential variation: Feel free to substitute Vegenaise®, your favorite non-GMO mayo or similar dressing, for the almond spread. You can also replace the fresh lemon juice with 1 drop pure lemon essential oil in 2 teaspoons purified water.

In 1896, New York's Waldorf-Astoria Hotel restaurant maître d' Oscar Tschirky created the original Waldorf Salad by spontaneously tossing together a concoction of apples and celery with mayonnaise.

Walnut Spread

1 cup walnuts, soaked, rinsed and well drained

1/2 Bartlett pear, chopped (about 1/2 cup)

1/4 cup fresh basil, packed

1 medium clove garlic, crushed

1 tablespoon non-GMO verified gluten-free tamari

1 tablespoon each fresh parsley and rosemary

1/4 teaspoon pink Himalayan salt

Pulse all ingredients in a food processor until well combined. Spread on crackers or sandwiches, or serve as a dip with veggies or your favorite wholesome chips.

Essential variation: For a heavenly treat, consider adding two drops pure tangerine essential oil.

Ancient folklore suggests that since the walnut meat within the shell resembles the wrinkled shape of the brain, that eating walnuts may stimulate the intellect.

About the Illustrator

Royce Richardson makes his home in Seattle, Washington where he designs and illustrates for several types of media, including books, film, and a series of personalized videos called Luminous Meditations.

Royce's formal training includes a B.A. in Fine Arts from Seattle University. In addition to being an artist, he is also an accomplished author and composer. His novel, "The Blissmaker," was awarded a Benjamin Franklin Award for Best Work of Fiction and was also voted Book of the Year by the Coalition of Visionary Retailers. The story of his novel is not unlike his own, as it reflects the spiritual journey of a composer.

His music CD, "MoonCrest," contains piano compositions that were created throughout his writing of the novel. You can hear examples of this music, and learn more about Royce's work by going to **Blissmaker.com**.

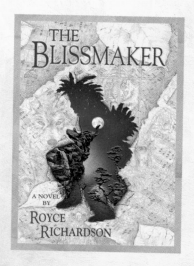

About the Author

Madeline Eyer is an internationally recognized Certified Raw Food Coach, Certified Holistic Health Coach, energetic healing practitioner, and Reiki Master. She has also studied sound healing, Theta Healing, metaphysical anatomy, and more. Madeline used raw food in conjunction with these healing modalities to restore her own health, and she uses these same tools to assist her clients in achieving soul-level healing.

Madeline's deep desire for spiritual evolution, her love of natural healing, and her sense of adventure have led her to expand her skills through visits to a number of the world's sacred sites. She has long had an affinity for working with flower essences and essential oils, often creating her own blends.

Currently, Madeline resides in the Seattle area with her husband, Mark, where they enjoy spending time in nature and growing their own vegetables.

Claim your free *3-Day Essential Raw Experience* at MadelineEyer.com.

Also by Madeline and Royce

Essential Green Smoothies

Quick, easy and delicious solutions for your healthy lifestyle

Available at
EssentialGreenSmoothies.com
MadelineEyer.com
and select retailers